Bonjour Eiffel Tower!

Bonjour Explorers.
Do you want to visit **Paris** with me?

First, let's count the neighborhoods, starting with 1, 2, 3.

In French it's called a **Boulangerie**.

Thankfully we rescued Little Dove.
His wing is not broken but could use some love.

Little Dove will join our adventure until his wing can carry him better.

Climbing the pipes of the **Pompidou**, we are able to get a better view.

Do you see the glass pyramids at the **Louvre**?

Inside lives the **Mona Lisa**,

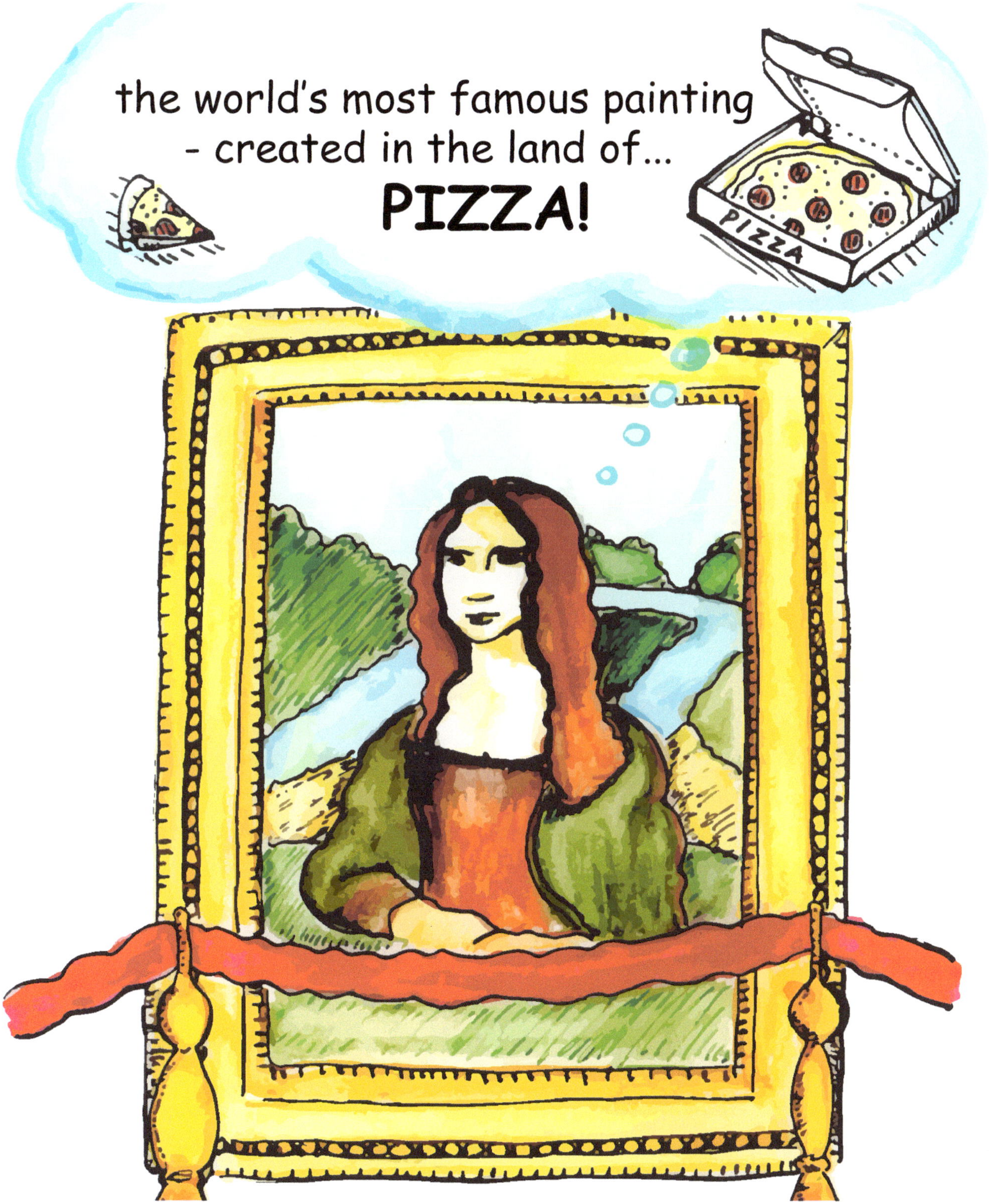
the world's most famous painting
- created in the land of...
PIZZA!
PIZZA

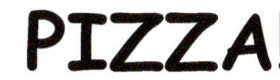

Green, yellow, red and blue,
each **métro** line can take us somewhere new.

While listening to the music by street musicians, they dive for picnic crumbs with precision.

Allez- let's go!
Here's a cool scooter we can drive;
put on your helmet as we go for a ride!

Also, in **Paris** we can go and float,
cruising upon a river boat!
The boat will take us to the **Eiffel Tower**,
whose lights will sparkle upon the hour.

Voila!
We made it to the **Eiffel Tower** on time.
Soon her bright lights will sparkle and shine!

The tower's light show is about to go live.
Help us count down, starting from five.

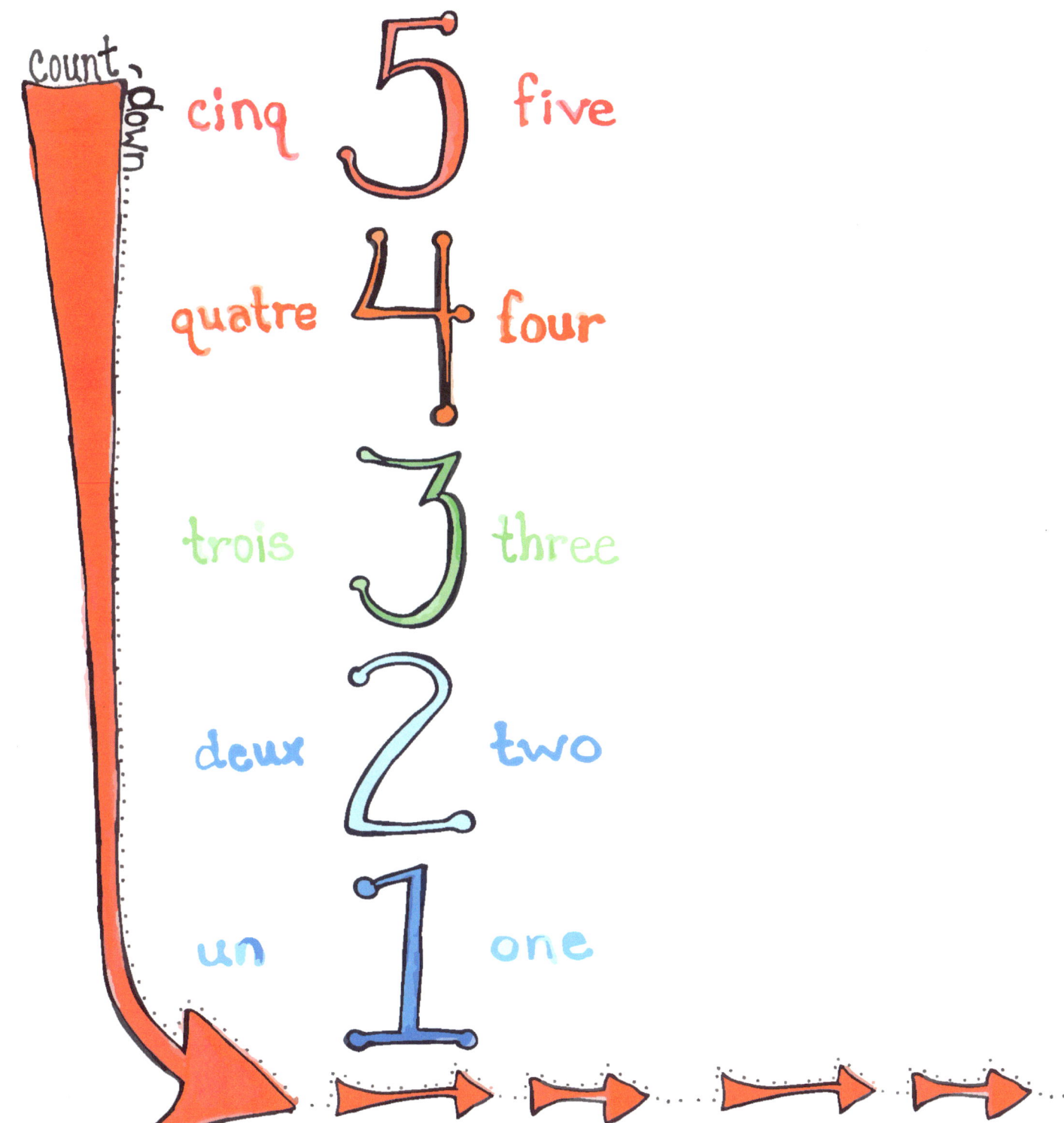

Little Explorers, can you count in French with me?

Un [uhn] = One

Deux [duh] = Two

Trois [trwah] = Three

Quatre [kah-truh] = Four

Cinq [sank] = Five

To access coloring sheets, music & activities visit us on our site below.

travelwithmeandsee.com

Share and tag your adventures with us...

 @travelwithmeandsee.kids

Adult Explorers, you can speak French too...allez!

Au revoir [oh ruh-vwahr] = Goodbye
À bientôt [ah bee-an-toh] = See you soon
Allez [ah-lay] = Let's go
Bonjour [bohn-zhoor] = Hello
Boulangerie [boo-lahn-zhuh-ree] = Bakery
Crêpe [krehp] = Thin pancake with fillings
Crêperie [krehp-eh-ree] = Street stand or café specializing in crêpes
Merci [mehr-see] = Thank you
Métro [may-troh] = Subway
Oui [wee] = Yes
Voilà [vwah-lah] = Here it is

Travel with Me & See *Petite* fun facts!

Eiffel Tower- built as a communications tower
France- a European country, smaller than the state of Texas
Louvre- one of the biggest museums in the world
Mona Lisa- painted by Leonardo da Vinci of Italy
Paris- the capital of France
Pompidou- a modern art museum
Sacré-Cœur Church- rests on Montmartre hill
Stravinsky Fountain- features 16 water sculptures

TRAVEL WITH ME & SEE

Petite

Next stop... LONDON

À BIENTÔT — SEE YOU SOON

Tick tock, tick tock...

Text Copyright © 2022 by Nancy Delevoye. Illustrations Copyright © 2022 by Carly Wadsworth. All rights reserved. No part of this book may be reproduced, transmitted or stored in an information retrieval system in any form or by any means, graphic, electronic or mechanical, including photocopying, taping and recording, without prior written permission from the publishers. First edition printed 2022. ISBN 978-0-9600423-4-0 (paperback)
This book was typeset in Comic Sans MS, Comic Sans MS - Bold and Futura. The illustrations were done with watercolor pencil, markers and ink. Self-published by Nancy Delevoye and Carly Wadsworth. Perpignan, France & Detroit, MI, USA.

Be Curious • Be an Explorer • Be a Child of the World • Be You!

 @travelwithmeandsee.kids

travelwithmeandsee.com

www.ingramcontent.com/pod-product-compliance
Lightning Source LLC
Chambersburg PA
CBHW042144290426
44110CB00002B/108